# Martin Bryant:

## The Port Arthur Massacre

by Jack Rosewood

**Historical Serial Killers and Murderers**

**True Crime by Evil Killers**

**Volume 9**

Copyright © 2015 by Wiq Media

ALL RIGHTS RESERVED

No part of this book may be reproduced, stored in a retrieval system, or transmitted in any form or by any means, electronic, mechanical, photocopying, recording, scanning, or otherwise, without the prior written permission of the publisher.

ISBN-13: 978-1519215956

# Contents

Prologue .................................................................1

**Chapter One:** The Odd Nature of Martin Bryant ..................6

**Chapter Two:** The Odd Couple ..............................................13

**Chapter Three:** The Café Massacre........................................21

**Chapter Four:** The Parking Lot ..............................................31

**Chapter Five:** Fleeing the Scene............................................37

**Chapter Six:** Road Rage ........................................................42

**Chapter Seven:** A Scene of Total Devastation ....................47

**Chapter Eight:** The Cornered Madman................................51

**Chapter Nine:** The Aftermath ...............................................59

**Chapter Ten:** Understanding the Mind of a Killer................65

Epilogue ..................................................................................73

More books by Jack Rosewood ...............................................78

A Note From The Author .......................................................84

# Prologue

There are few spots on the earth that have the brutal and equally fascinating history of Port Arthur, located in the Australian province of Tasmania. First settled by the British in 1830, it served from 1833 to 1877 as an "escape proof prison" for England's most notorious and dangerous criminals. With these Penal Colonies, the logic was simple - by sending convicted prisoners far across the ocean to the British controlled territory of Australia, there would be no risk of these criminals ever committing crimes at home again and was considered a fitting punishment for their acts.

For more than four decades, Port Arthur served as a high security prison that many of those who entered, would never leave alive. Officially, 1646 men lost their lives in Port Arthur including 180 guards who had the unfortunate luck to be stationed there. Conditions were deplorable and hunger was both a weapon and a lethal deterrent.

In modern times, the prison has been maintained by the Australian Government and is considered an important historical landmark representing the heritage of the country. The majority of main prison itself stills stands as a haunting reminder of those that were imprisoned there and subjected to harsh and brutal treatment - with no hope of escape.

For prisoners that were lucky enough to make it over the walls of the penitentiary, there was nowhere to go. The waters surrounding the area were swarming with sharks including great whites, and the unhospitable Tasmanian countryside was more dangerous than any threat one would face inside the prison. There were no cities or towns to run to – just hundreds of square miles of unhospitable wilderness. For many prisoners, their only way out was death and it was not uncommon to murder another prisoner in order to receive a death sentence from the warden which was preferable to living out your life within the walls of Port Arthur.

Nearly 150 years later Port Arthur has become a popular tourist attraction that has drawn people from all over the world. Surrounded by ocean and jagged rocks, the area is stunningly beautiful and many of the surviving buildings have been restored and maintained. Tourists can explore the prison and the rugged coastline or take a trip out to the Isle of the Dead where many of the prisoners were buried after dying from starvation or horrid work conditions imposed by sadistic prison guards and wardens.

In 1996, the parking lots would fill daily with hundreds of cars and tour busses from around Tasmania, bringing in curious tourists anxious to see this hauntingly stunning piece of history. A popular café and gift shop called the Broad Arrow Cafe offered both a place to get something to eat and to purchase a souvenir for visitors to take home.

There was no reason for anyone to suspect on April 28, 1996, was going to be a day any different from any other at the site. The sky was clear and the air still crisp as the multitude of tourists arrived as they did every day to explore the area. No one would suspect that shortly after 1:30 p.m., a lone crazed gunman, angry at society as a whole - would pull out a semi-automatic rifle and begin shooting every living person he would see. The event was made even more shocking in that it had taken place just a few weeks after 27 people were killed in Dunblane, Scotland, where a crazed gunman had also shocked the world. It was suggested the Port Arthur event was the act of a copycat shooter – but as police and investigators would later learn, the Australian gunman was completely unpredictable and had a long, bizarre past.

For those outside of Australia, few remember the brutal attack in which 35 people were gunned down in cold blood by 28 year old Martin John Bryant. Without warning or indication, the disturbed wayward young man woke up that April Sunday morning, loaded a duffle bag with several semi-automatic rifles and proceeded to the historic tourist destination. Upon his arrival, he systematically executed men, woman and children with a level of cold blooded callousness that had rarely been seen before; which is part of what makes this tale so shocking. To this day, it represents one of the largest mass shootings in world history committed by a lone gunman.

For those that have tried to make sense of what is now known as the "Port Arthur Massacre" there is still relatively little known about what caused Martin Bryant to commit such mass murder. There are those that insist that Bryant didn't do the shootings at all - and was set up by a government plot to regulate gun ownership in Australia.

For those though that survived the massacre, they are forever haunted by the vision of those around them being gunned down without reason or mercy. The lives that were lost added to the long history of where so many had died more than a century before them.

The murderous rampage that took place at Port Arthur defied reason and shocked even the most seasoned investigators. This is the story as told by the survivors as well as the investigators who were given the task of trying to understand one simple question – why did Martin Bryant wake up one morning and kill 35 people he didn't know?

This is the story of the Port Arthur Massacre, Australia's worst mass murder in history.

## Chapter One:

# The Odd Nature of Martin Bryant

Reaching over to turn off his alarm clock, Martin Bryant opened his eyes, rolled over in his bed and looked briefly at his girlfriend Petra who was still sleeping beside him. He sat up and gained his bearings, then stretching, he stood up and walked to his dresser where he pulled a shirt on. It was Sunday, April 28, 1996 and the sun was already shining brightly outside.

For everyone else it was just another April weekend – but for him - today was special - today was the day he would make things right.

The idea of committing mass murder had occurred to him nearly three months prior during an alcohol fueled period when he was drinking an entire bottle of Bailey's Irish Crème and Sambuca on a daily basis. The anti-depressants his doctor had prescribed had little effect on his state of mind and he felt a growing anger do to the way people shunned him when he tried to talk to them. More and more the thought of shooting people not only fascinated him – but gave him comfort and a sense of calmness.

For years he felt as though life was against him. Everything that seemed so right and important in his simple mind was now gone. His close and eccentric friend, Helen Harvey had died after their car swerved into on-coming traffic. He would survive the crash – one that many would blame him for causing.

Ten months later, his father, Maurice Bryant would commit suicide after suffering from a long bout of depression brought on by his son's growingly bizarre behavior. Upon his father's death, Martin Bryant lost his only real anchor and the one person able to control him that he had in his life. It had become a full time job for his father to keep him out of trouble and now no one was there to stop him from doing as he pleased.

As the months passed, he felt a growing anger inside him towards not just life but people in general. His mother struggled to understand him - she didn't have the same control that her husband did when it came to her son. Growing up he had been labelled as "annoying and difficult" and as an adult had a great deal of difficulty keeping any sort of employment; as he had very little ability to get along with others.

Martin Bryant was only 6 years old when he first caught the attention of a school psychologist who was concerned over reports that he had been torturing animals. As a child he was continually bullied by other children for being so different and he had no ability to interact with other kids. It was not uncommon for him to spend an entire school day with his face contorted, for no apparent reason, like he had eaten something sour. As he began to grow older, he began to take his aggression out on those younger than him and was soon transferred to New Town High School where they had a special needs program more adept at handling his difficult personality and behavior patterns.

At age 14, his father bought the young teen an air rifle which he later would claim was the worst decision of his life. Bryant became fascinated with the weapon and was caught several times hiding in the bushes along the highway where he would shoot at passing motorists. In on particularly alarming incident involving the gun, he shot a parrot out of a tree and while is lay incapacitated on the ground – he walked up and shot it point blank in the head several times until it was dead.

By the time he left school, psychiatrists had noted that his IQ tested at 68 - which classified him as mentally retarded. Because he could neither read or write as an adult, the Australian Government issued him a long term disability pension. In his early 20's, he took odd jobs around New Town and the City of Hobart as a gardener and handyman.

Months before his murderous rampage he told a startled neighbor that one day "I'll do something that will make everyone remember me." For months he had been planning his attack - and now he was determined today was going to be the day when that came true. A few weeks earlier, he purchased a green duffle bag large enough to carry several boxes of ammunition, as well as, two semi-automatic rifles and an assault shotgun. With the bag loaded, he slung it over his shoulder, turned on the alarm system to his house and headed to his yellow Volvo parked out front.

It was 9:47 am.

In 1993, Martin Bryant had bought his first real gun – an AR-10 semi-automatic rifle from a local gun store and over the next three years would purchase numerous other rifles – including a 12 gauge Daewoo shot gun, as well as, a Colt AR-15 carbine assault rifle. The AR-15 is the same rifle as the M16 used by the United States Marines. The only distinguishing difference is that it is not automatic but is still capable of firing 30 consecutive rounds before needing to reload.

During this period, he also purchased a L1A1 SLR-308 caliber battle rifle that was popular with ground troops in the British, Canadian and Australian armies. The rifle held 30, 51 mm steal jacket armor piercing bullets that could be fired in rapid succession and was capable of piercing through brick, wood and steel. The shells were based on the famous 308 Winchester bullet.

With hundreds of rounds of ammunition loaded in his bag and three deadly assault rifles – Bryant began his 45 minute journey down the Arthur highway, through Forcett Village and then to a bed and breakfast called Seascape, which was less than 15 minutes from the famous Port Arthur historical site.

Seascape had bitter sweet meaning to Martin Bryant. His father Maurice had tried to purchase the property, but before he could finalize financing, the property was bought by David Martin and his wife Noelene. The elder Bryant was furious and bitterly complained that they had only bought the bed and breakfast out of spite and to hurt his family. His son listened intently and harbored the same resentment towards the couple – and who years later he would blame for his father's suicide.

Arriving at Sea Scape shortly before noon he opened the trunk of his car, took out the loaded AR-15 rifle and walked into the front entrance of the Inn; where seeing Noelene Martin, he shot the woman several times, killing her. As David Martin came running to see what had happened, Bryant shot the man knocking him to the ground. Gagging him with a wash cloth, he took a large knife from the kitchen counter and stabbed the man several times until he was dead.

A score had been settled and yet, this was only the beginning.

As he wiped the blood from his hands, he headed out of the building towards his car when a couple approached wanting to know if there were any accommodations available. He immediately told them that this would be completely impossible as his parents were away and his girlfriend was inside. The couple, shocked by his demeanor and odd behavior left the property quickly – unaware of just how close they had come to being his next victims.

Despite his simple nature, Martin Bryant's plan had gone as he expected; except for the meddling tourists who had nearly caught him killing the Martins. Undeterred, he backed his car up to the house and unloaded several boxes of ammunition. It was here that he planned to make his last stand after he had become the most famous man in Australia – for when he was done - no one would ever forget the name Martin Bryant.

Locking the doors to the building with the keys he had taken from the pocket of the dead owner, he walked purposefully to his car, started it and continued his journey to the busiest place he could think of – Port Arthur - where he knew hundreds of people would be already gathered on a busy Sunday afternoon.

Chapter Two:

## **The Odd Couple**

Hobart is the capital of Tasmania and was home to the eccentric Helen Harvey. At 54 years old, she was heir to the Tattersall's Lottery fortune – a for profit lottery business that had been operating in Australia since 1895 and was set up to share the substantial profits with the families of those that worked for the company.

She lived in a large mansion that was in significant need of repair, and with no one caring for the tall grass around the property, the 19 year old Martin Bryant approached her to see if she was interested in hiring him to mow the grass. Helen was happy to have the help and the two struck up an immediate friendship that would last until her death several years later. Bryant became a fixture at her home, helping feed the 14 dogs she kept inside and the 40 plus cats that lived in the garage.

The match was an odd one – but a close relationship bloomed and the young Bryant moved into the mansion. The couple would spend their days shopping and having dinner in some of Hobart's nicest restaurants all while buying more than 30 new cars as well as numerous other luxury purchases over the next 3 years.

City bylaw officers had received dozens of complaints from neighbors regarding the state of the property and the amount of animals being kept by the owners - and a cleanup order was issued for the mansion. When officials discovered the large amount of dogs and cats on the property, Hobart authorities issued an injunction preventing the couple from keeping any animals. This led to the purchase of a 72 acre farm called Taurusville in 1991, which was located in a community of Copping – approximately half way between where the mansion was located and the Port Arthur historic site.

Those in Copping quickly noticed the odd couple that was now part of their community. It wasn't uncommon to see one of their many cars parked outside local restaurants filled with animals including dogs, cats and even miniature ponies.

There were also growing concerns about the mental state of Bryant who had shot at several tourists with his pellet gun while they were buying apples from a nearby roadside stand. When police responded, they learned that he had often been spotted at night roaming the area with the gun shooting at dogs and passing cars. Upon their request, psychiatrists examined the trouble man who told them he often fantasized about shooting people. It was determined though that as long as he was under his father's watch, he did not present more than a nuisance danger to the public. Needless to say -those in the area avoided him because his nature was too unpredictable.

Two years had now passed since Helen and Martin had moved to the farm, and in late October, while driving into town, the car the couple was in suddenly swerved into oncoming traffic and struck a vehicle head on; killing Helen instantly. Martin was taken by ambulance with serious head and back injuries spent the next 7 months recovering in the hospital in Hobart.

During the investigation, police learned that Helen Harvey had already had three accidents caused by Martin lunging at the steering wheel while she was driving. She also told friends that she was careful never to drive too fast when he was in the car as she never knew when he would try and grab the wheel. With Helen Harvey now deceased, there was no witness or evidence to prove that Bryant had in fact purposely caused the crash. Thus, it was ruled an accident. What was clear to those around Bryant was that he had no ability to either restrain himself from sudden impulsive and dangerous acts – or the ability to understand the consequences of his actions.

As her closest friend, the eccentric Harvey had left her entire estate to Bryant, who now found himself worth over a half million dollars as the owner of both the farm in Copping and the Mansion back in Hobart. Since he had no financial sense or capacity to understand math, Martin Bryant's mother applied to have his affairs legally transferred to her as a guardian; knowing full well that her simple and troubled son would squander the money on who knew what.

While Bryant was still recovering from the accident nearly a year earlier, his father had to quit his job to take care of the farm full time. In June of 1993, Martin was released from the hospital and two months later, Maurice Bryant was discovered dead in a dam reservoir. Police had been searching the property after a neighbor found a note pinned to the door saying to call the police. No one had seen Maurice Bryant for days.

Officer Phil Pyke was one of the constables involved in the search. He would later recall that Bryant showed little interest in looking for his missing father. Police had determined that a shotgun was missing from the property and had begun to suspect that the clinically depressed man may have used the weapon to cause harm to himself. The initial search began up the hill of the property and through the bushes that lead up to the Tasmania back country. With no sign of the missing man, the search focused on the house and outbuildings around the property where police hoped to find a clue as to where the missing man might be.

Police began to make note of the young man with long blond hair that stood along the fence line and watched the female officers intently. They knew that the strange young man lived on the property and was the son of the man they were looking for, but he seemed far more interested in asking the women constables out to dinner than he did about the whereabouts of his missing father. During their investigation, Police had found Maurice Bryant's car parked in a shed and large sums of money lay strewn about the kitchen in the house. This only served to make the situation even more bizarre.

A search of the property turned up nothing and it was only after police divers were called in did they find Maurice Bryant at the bottom of the reservoir with several weights tied around his body. These weights helped drag his body to the bottom of the pond, making it more difficult for searchers to find. In addition to the dead man, divers also found several sheep carcasses who had apparently also drowned – a finding that puzzled police as sheep were not known to drink from bodies of water like the one they found Maurice Bryant in, and rarely, if ever would fall in.

Martin Bryant showed little emotion when divers found his drowned father and he was called upon to identify his body. He stood motionless for a moment looking at the corpse before nodding to Constable Garry Whittle that is was in fact his dad. He then walked away laughing to himself and seemed completely disconnected from the situation or the death of his father. As Martin returned to the house, the local water truck arrived and he proceeded to talk jovially with the driver, laughing loudly and telling him a new joke he had heard a few days prior – all while completely ignoring the police activity down at the dam.

Police had once again found themselves investigating yet another odd situation where Martin Bryant's name came up. Investigators were suspicious of Bryant's involvement in the death, but the coroner declared the death a suicide after the investigation revealed numerous indications that Maurice Bryant had suffered from depression, and had in fact taken his own life. Many suspected that the sheer weight of trying to deal with his irrational and bizarre son was too much to bare and suicide was his only way out.

Upon Maurice Bryant's death, the younger Bryant inherited another $250,000.

With both his father and close friend now dead, there was no one to keep Martin Bryant from becoming even more and more odd - and his behavior became increasingly bizarre and unpredictable.

Town residents would recall that he would walk about town in a straw Panama hat and shiny lizard skinned shoes, dressed in grey linen suit and carrying a leather brief case telling anyone who would listen about his success as a business man. At night, he would go to dinner by himself wearing an electric blue suit and bothering those that sat around him.

With Helen and his father dead - his despair continued to grow and he became suicidal. He travelled extensively after his father's death, often hoping to find a country where people would be friendlier to him. In total he took 14 such trips but finally gave up looking for a better place to be – telling his doctor that the only thing he enjoyed about travelling abroad was the conversations he would have with those forced to sit beside him on the long plane rides. In late 1995, he told his mother that he had "had enough of how people treated him and he was tired of feeling like everyone was against him"

But then an idea occurred to him.

An unforgettable way to get even with those that had so often dismissed him and treated him badly – and despite his meager intellect, a plan began to form. One thing was for certain, he would need more ammunition then he had on hand.

## Chapter Three:

# The Café Massacre

With the Martin's barely dead a half hour, Bryant headed past Port Arthur and up to an area called Palmer's Lookout Road where the couple had a home overlooking the ocean. Along the way he approached a tourist's car that had over heated along the road and slowed down to talk to the two people beside the vehicle. "You should come up to the café at Port Arthur" he told them "and have a coffee."

Upon arriving at the driveway of the Martin's home, Roger Larner, a neighbor of the Martin's greeted him and the two men engaged in small talk. Bryant told the man he was thinking about buying the Martin's home and asked whether he thought they would mind if he was to take a closer at the house. Larner had met Bryant several years prior and knew him to be unpredictable and odd – so he said he would come along with Bryant up to the property while he looked at it. The young man suddenly changed his mind and said he would be back later that afternoon after he took care of a few things. He then got into his car and began heading back to Port Arthur.

***

When Bryant arrived at Port Arthur there was little outside of his long wavy blonde hair to distinguish him from the hundreds of other people that were arriving in the parking lot. It was lunch time and the clear skies and the warm sun had brought out the tourists which made parking difficult.

As the security manager at Port Arthur, Ian Kingston was in charge that day of directing traffic as it arrived into the site. He paused to talk with Bryant as he arrived. The driver asked if he could park down close to the café, but Kingston told him that he should go over to the main parking lot. Bryant then countered if it would be alright if he parked in front of the information center rather than farther away from the cafe. Again he was told to go to the main parking lot. He did for a few minutes before driving back up and parking on the other side of the busses, close to the Broad Arrow café – a popular restaurant and gift shop enjoying a brisk afternoon of business thanks to the nice weather.

Kingston noticed that he had moved his car despite what he had been told, but decided not to bother confronting the man who seemed rather odd. He watched Bryant open the trunk of his car and take out a greenduffle bag of which he slung over his shoulder and walked into the café. With cars still pouring in from the highway, he returned his attention to directing traffic.

Bryant found himself hungry and he ordered lunch from the pretty girl behind the counter. His habit of talking in a near whimsical voice like he was out of a sixties surfing movie was barely noticed in the rush of customers ordering their meals. Taking his food outside, he sat by himself at a table and ate his lunch, talking to those around him in a mumbling, often incoherent voice. To one couple, he mentioned the lack of Japanese tourists and with another man he struck up a short conversation about the amount of yellow jacket wasps in the area.

Standing up, he picked up his tray and walked back into the café with his duffle bag. Putting his dishes down on an empty table, he calmly reached into his bag and took out a video camera which he set up towards the crowd – wanting to ensure that what he was about to do was captured forever on video tape. He then took out the still bloody knife he had used to stab David Martin to death and placed it on the table.

The café was small and crowded and many of the tables were close together. More than 60 people were in the building when Bryant reached into his bag and took out the loaded Colt AR 15 semi-automatic assault rifle. He then pointed at two tourists from Malaysia - Moh Yee Ng and Sou Leng Chung. Pulling the trigger, the bullets ripped into couple and they died instantly.

Turning to the man standing to his left, he fired again, grazing the head of Mike Sargent who immediately fell to the floor dazed but still alive. Bryant continued to shoot, this time striking a fatal blow to the back of the head of Sargent's girlfriend, Kate Elizabeth Scott, who was killed instantly.

Panic swept across the café as people tried to dive for cover or get out of the crowded area. In a desperate attempt to distract Bryant, 28-year-old Jason Winter threw his tray at the gunman as his wife Joanne dove for cover with the couple's 15 month old child.

Outside the café, Security Manager Ian Kingston - who had directed Bryant as to where to park only twenty minutes earlier - could hear the sharp pops of what at first he thought was an electrical fire. As he walked quickly towards the café he could see clouds of dust and smoke coming from the door and the continual sound of what he began to realize was likely gun fire. As he began to run towards the front entrance of the cafe, he could now hear the terrified screams of those inside.

Inside, the carnage continued and Anthony Nightingale barely had time to yell "No – not here" before Bryant aimed his rifle at him and shot him through the neck, killing him on the spot. Bryant reached into his pocket and loaded another magazine of bullets into the gun.

Across the room, a group of elderly tourists had pulled their tables together to accommodate the ten of them for lunch; including Peter Croswell who had just finished eating when the shooting began. Instinctively, he tried to shield his friends from the gunfire, pulling Thelma Walker and Pamela Law to the ground and out of direct fire of Bryant's deadly onslaught. His instinctive efforts were unable to protect 68 year old Kevin Sharp who was killed instantly after being shot close range.

Another member of their group, Walter Bennett was shot in the back, and the bullet ripped through him, striking Raymond Sharp and killing both men. Others in the group including John and Gaye Fidler, as well as, Gerald Broome and Patricia Barker were all struck by bullet fragments. The four would survive the massacre but be forever scarred by the terrifying memory of the look on the face of the crazed cold blooded killer who was shooting at anyone in his path.

As Kingston approached the Broad Arrow Café from the outside, he had no idea what to expect as he neared the door. The first thing he saw was a man bleeding profusely at the entrance who appeared to be dead. The scene inside was absolute carnage, and Bryant was still firing on the crowd with his back to Kingston who was unarmed and unable to fight back. Kingston arrived just as Tony Kistan stood up from his seat and was hit in the head with a bullet causing his face to nearly disintegrate - but not before he was able to push his wife Sarah to the ground and to safety. His friend Andrew Mills was struck from less than 6 feet away with a deadly shot to the head and he also died instantly.

Ian Kingston turned from the door and ran back across the parking lot yelling for tourists to follow him to cover. Many outside the cafe originally thought the gunfire was part of a reenactment being put on by museum staff – by the time they realized that the gunfire was real it would be too late for many of them.

As the sound of gun fire continued inside the café, those within ear shot began to move back from the building and towards Kingston's yelling; while others moved closer, wanting to see what was going on and what all the noise was about.

There was not obvious escape from the building as Bryant blocked the main entrance and was shooting at whoever moved. Graham Colver was struck in the jaw by a bullet from Bryant's rifle, and would barely survive choking on his own blood from the wound. Colver's wife Carolyn was shot in the back but would survive the attack – her daughter Sarah Loughton was killed instantly after she was struck in the head by a bullet from the AR-15 Rifle.

Mervyn Howard barely had time to move before Bryant killed him with a fatal blast that travelled through his body and out the window of the café shattering the glass – the first real sign to those outside that something truly terrible was happening inside.

The gunman then turned to Howard's wife Mary who he shot in the neck. As she lay dying on the floor, Bryant stood above her, paused and then shot her point blank in the head – much like he had to the parrot when he was 14 years old.

With most everyone in the café either dead or lying injured, Bryant then moved towards the attached gift shop where he would continue to shoot at unsuspecting tourists who had no escape. A door at the back of the building was locked and there was nowhere to run.

Barely 45 seconds had passed and 12 people were now dead with another 10 laying wounded on the floor of the cafe including Robert Elliott who was shot in the arm and head but was still alive near the fireplace.

Two employees behind the front counter were shot and killed as Bryant started to move into the attached gift shop adjacent to the dining area in the café. Nicole Burgess, who was just 17 and working part time at the café counter was killed instantly after she was struck in the head with a direct shot from Bryant's gun. Elizabeth Howard, 26, was hit twice, once in the arm and a second shot in the chest which killed her.

By now, a complete sense of terror and panic swept over the entire building as the gunman continued to fire indiscriminately at anyone or anything that moved. Tourists dove for cover behind whatever they could find – but the wooden tables were no match for the steel tipped armor piercing bullets being fired from Bryant's rifle. Corallee Lever hid, terrified to move and unable to help her husband Dennis who lay dying on the floor after being shot in the head.

By the rear locked exit, Peter Nash lay on top of his wife Carolyn in an attempt to shield her from the gun fire. Close by, Pauline Masters and Ron Jary had been unable to get the door open and now crouched in the corner terrified that the gunman would see them.

Gwen Neander was still trying desperately to open the locked door and was immediately shot from behind by Bryant, striking her in the head and killing her on the spot. Bryant then began to move into the gift shop and shot at an overturned table, striking Peter Crosswell in the buttock – the table offering little defense against the bullets which ripped through the wood as if it wasn't there. The gunman then stopped to reload his rifle giving a brief pause in the carnage as the shooting briefly paused.

Tourist Jason Winter mistakenly assumed the attack was over after he heard no more shooting and stood up just as Bryant had finished putting a fresh clip into his AR-15. Winter was shot as he held his hands up to protect himself - the bullet passed through his hand striking him in the chest and neck. A second shot hit him in the face and he collapsed to the floor dead. On the floor behind Winter, Dennis Olson and his wife Mary, who had been vacationing in Australia from the United States were wounded by bullet fragments but both would survive.

With next to no movement in the gift shop, Bryant turned and started to walk to the front entrance of the café. As he made his way through the maze of dead bodies, overturned tables and chairs, he saw Ronald Jary, Peter Nash and Pauline Masters who were hiding and had been able to avoid being shot in the first wave of the attack. He coldly shot all three, killing the trio in a hail of gun fire. To the left, Bryant spotted an Asian tourist who had nowhere to hide or escape to – but Bryant's rifle was empty and he had no more clips in his coat pockets.

The crazed gunman moved back towards the table where his bag had been left, reloaded his rifle, and put the strap of the duffle bag over his shoulder before walking out onto the deck of the café.

Less than three minutes had passed and 20 people were now dead, with another 12 laying severely wounded by the attack.

Chapter Four:

# The Parking Lot

Although the sound of gun fire had been echoing across the grounds and was originating from the café, most outside had very little idea of what was happening. In the front of the café, Ian Kingston was yelling for those in the parking lot to follow him to cover. Behind the building, several employees had escaped out through the back kitchen exit and were motioning for those they could see to take cover. For those in the vicinity, the entire situation was very surreal and no one seemed quite sure what the commotion was about - or whether it was part of a reenactment taking place for tourists. The popping noise from inside the building had stopped and barely five minutes had passed since the sound had begun.

As Bryant stepped out into the sunlight on onto the deck of the café where only a few minutes ago, he had been eating his lunch – he pointed his gun and squeezed off several shots at Ashley John Law who was attempting to move tourists to safety across the parking lot some 100 yards away. The bullets narrowly missed them as zipped by and struck the trees. The sound of gun fire echoed across the lot, and for the first time, both tourists and employees began to truly realize the severity of the situation.

Since the parking lot was full of large tour buses, those who were still on the pavement saw the gunman standing on the deck of the café and heard the shots. One of the coach drivers, Royce Thompson was the first to come into the direct line of Bryant's fire and was shot in the back as he tried to run between two buses to safety. Bleeding, he fell to the ground and rolled under the bus. He would later die of his injuries and would be murder victim number 21 of the massacre.

As Bryant moved towards the other buses he shot Brigid Cook in the thigh as she was attempting to tell people to run for safety. The bullet shattered her femur bone so severely that fragments of the bone wounded coach driver Ian McElwee. Both would recover from their injuries and survive the assault.

As the crowd of people still in the open moved to the rear of the buses for some form of cover - Bryant shot at them indiscriminately before turning his attention to another coach where tourists were screaming as they scrambled to get out of his line of fire. Just as Winifred Aplin was about to get around the back corner of the bus, she was struck by a bullet in her side. She collapsed and died before rescuers could reach her. Yvonne Lockley was more fortunate – a bullet grazed her face and despite being terrified and in pain, she was able to get into one of the open buses and take cover where Bryant was unable to see her.

Confusion reigned supreme as Bryant continued to systematically shoot at anything he saw moving. A group of tourists made the mistake of turning back towards the bus area after they were misinformed that they were fleeing in the wrong direction - they nearly ran right into Bryant who opened fire on them. Janet Quin, a Wildlife Park owner, was shot in the back and lay helpless on the tarmac. Doug Hutchinson was wounded in the arm but continued to run for cover until he found a place to hide and was able to avoid being injured any further.

As Bryant moved along the coast line of the cove, he approached his car and opened up the hatchback where he changed rifles. Dropping the AR 15 into car, he took out a FN FAL – a semi-automatic rifle capable of firing up to 700 rounds a minute. The weapon was popular with most NATO military forces and was readily available to gun collectors thanks to the more than 2 million rifles in circulation. The clip held 30, 308 rounds and was known for its reliability in combat and its accuracy at long distances.

Now re-armed, he fired at the tourists who stood across the main field between the bus parking and the main wall of the penitentiary ruins — but did not strike anyone.

Seemingly content that there were no more victims to be killed — Bryant climbed into his car only to reemerge and head directly back towards the cluster of parked buses where he spotted more tourists frantically trying to hide from him. When they realized he was coming for them, they ran frantically towards the buses as he open fired on them.

As Bryant drew closer to the first bus in his path, he came upon the wounded Janet Quin. Laying helpless and face down on the tarmac, he shot her from close range in the back and killed her.

He then walked around the coach, stepping into the open door and up the steps of the bus where he spotted Elva Gaylard trying to hide a few rows back in the bus. Calmly pointing his assault rifle at her, he shot her in the chest and killed her instantly. Still standing in the aisle of the bus, Bryant could see Gordon Francis attempting to close the door of the adjacent coach and he shot him through the glass. Although seriously wounded, Francis would survive his injuries.

Bryant then stepped of the bus where he encountered Neville Quin - the husband of Janet Quin. He chased the man around the coach and fired two rounds in his pursuit before catching up to him and pointing the rifle directly in his face.

"No one gets away from me" Bryant said in his almost comical surfer voice. Realizing the gunman was about to the pull the trigger, Quin jolted his body away from the rifle barrel but was struck in the neck rendering him momentarily paralyzed. Bryant assumed the man was dead and didn't fire again allowing Quin to crawl over to his wounded wife where she died a few minutes later in his arms. Although bleeding from his neck, Neville Quin would survive and recover from his wounds.

Bryant continued to fire at anyone he saw moving. For those in the area, there seemed to be no escape and the echoes of the shots being fired made it difficult to determine where they were coming from. Barely 10 minutes had passed and 24 people were now dead with another 18 severely wounded.

Walking back over to his car, Bryant climbed into the driver's seat, closed the door and started the vehicle. However, his murderous spree wasn't over yet.

Chapter Five:

# Fleeing the Scene

911 emergency phone lines were now jammed as frantic callers reported the events in progress at Port Arthur. The closest main Police detachment was in the city of Hobart almost an hour away from the historical site. Operators could barely make out the panicked callers voices as they reported a gunman shooting at tourists – all while in the background the sounds of gun fire could be heard. Only two officers were in the area and were attending a false alarm at Saltwater River – about 14 miles from Port Arthur. It was 1:36 pm.

As word of the attack spread, doctors at the Royal Hobart Hospital began to try and interpret the fragmented reports of mass causalities and multiple gunshot victims from Port Arthur. Nothing had been confirmed yet but across the city the sound of police and ambulance sirens dominated the sleepy afternoon as first responders raced to reach Port Arthur.

Now leaving the parking lot, Martin Bryant drove his car along the tree lined road where he approached Nanette Mikac and her two young children, 3 year old Madeline and 6 year old Alannah. The Mikac's had been hiding with Museum Security Manager Ian Kingston – but had decided it would be safer to try and run from the area rather than hide with the large group of tourists Kingston had rounded up. Despite the man's pleas for her to stay, she began running down the road and now was face to face with the crazed gunman who she originally assumed was someone stopping to offer her help.

Bryant stepped out of the car just as someone yelled "It's him" and Nanette Mikac realized who she now faced. Putting his hand on the woman's shoulder, he told her to get on her knees of which she did. She begged the man not to harm her children. Ignoring her request – he put the rifle to her temple and fired – killing her instantly. He then turned towards 3 year old Madeline and shot her in the shoulder before shooting her a second time in the chest and killing the young girl. Alannah instinctively tried to run for safety and hid behind a tree where Bryant found her –

pushed the barrel of the rifle to her neck and pulled the trigger – killing the 6 year old.

Being a Sunday, the site was crowded with tourists and there were plenty of witnesses to the murder of the young family. Those close by began to run away from the scene and Bryant fired shots towards them but failed to hit anyone.

Hearing the gun shots in the direction of the road that the Mikac family had headed down, Ian Hamilton called up to the toll booth at the end of the road Bryant was on in an effort to try and warn others that the gunman was making his way towards them. When the attendant answered, he told her to get down on the floor and not to get up for any reason. The woman protested that she couldn't leave the money unattended and he told her "Don't worry about the bloody money, just get down on the floor".

As Nanette Mikac and her two daughters lay dead on the road, Bryant climbed into his car and headed back towards the toll booth of the park. As confusion compounded, others up towards the booth told drivers that they needed to leave the area as there was a crazed man shooting tourists down the road. The cars began to try and back up the winding tree lined road towards the toll booth – not knowing that Bryant was coming directly towards them. Others hid in the bushes and prayed that they wouldn't be seen. No one knew where Bryant was or what his next move would be.

In the panic, the narrow road and toll booth area had become blocked with confused drivers. One vehicle, a yellow BMW driven by Russell Pollard sat waiting for a way to turn around and get away from the area when Bryant approached them in his own car and got out – pointing the rifle at them.

Pollard and Mary Nixon sat frozen in the front seat while passengers Helene and Robert Salzmann were in the back seat. Bryant was walking towards the car when Robert Salzmann stepped out of the car and confronted the gunman. The two men exchanged angry words before Bryant pointed his rifle at him and shot him at point blank range – killing him on the spot. Russell Pollard stepped from the driver's seat and was shot in the chest from close range, a wound that would also prove to be fatal.

The two women, still inside the car, were heard as Bryant executed them at close range. He then pulled their bodies from the car left them on the road as horrified tourist watched in disbelief – many trapped in their own cars. Cars backed up frantically from the toll booth terrified they would be next. The gunman then calmly walked over to his own car, took out several boxes of ammunition, a set of handcuffs, his AR 15 rifle and a container of gasoline and put it into the BMW.

As he was about to get into the car, Graham Sutherland approached in his vehicle and Bryant opened fired – shattering the glass of the door, with another bullet puncturing the metal. Sutherland was able to put the car into reverse and escape the scene, before he was hit again.

Bryant climbed into the tourist's BMW, closed the door and sped off down the road towards the highway that lead back to the Bed and Breakfast in Seacape. His death toll now was at 31 men, women and children – and another 19 wounded.

## Chapter Six:

# Road Rage

As Bryant drove the stolen BMW back towards Seascape, emergency response vehicles were racing towards Port Arthur. There was no way to tell how many people had been involved, or who the gunman was – or even if there was more than one shooter. Back at the main museum area there had been no sound of gunshots for several minutes and people cautiously started to come out of hiding although still terrified at the prospect of more shots being fired.

Back in Hobart, medical staff were told to start preparing for multiple causalities and several trauma teams were being formed. Nurses cleared out an entire ward to deal with the wounded that were expected to be arriving via ambulance and helicopter. They had no idea how many to expect or what had actually happened – just to be ready for the worst.

Senior negotiator Terry McCarthy was on shift at the Hobart Police Station when the call came in. The call was from the tactical response team. The switchboard operator passed on a brief message to McCarthy - "20 dead at Port Arthur – get here now"

Having no idea what was going on, he immediately headed to his car and began the drive up to historical site along with every available police officer in the area.

***

The people mulling about the Mobil gas station on the main highway to Port Arthur had little idea of what had happened down at the museum site and were unprepared when Graham Sutherland approached with the glass missing from the side of his car and the bullet hole in the door. Sutherland yelled for people to take cover and told anyone who would listen of the crazed gunman who had murdered several people at the Port Arthur toll booth. People were unsure whether to believe the driver or dismiss him as some sort of lunatic.

Shortly behind Sutherland, a yellow BMW pulled in front of the driveway and blocked the path of white Toyota Corolla trying to leave. Bryant jumped out of his car and pointed the gun at the driver – demanding he get out of the car. The driver, Glenn Pears, held his hands up and begged the gunman not to hurt his girlfriend, Zoe Hall who was in the passenger seat of the car. Bryant grabbed Pears and dragged him towards the stolen car and forced him into the trunk where he shut the lid and locked him in. Walking back towards the Corolla, he looked at the pretty woman in the bright red blouse and black sweater as she tried to climb over to the driver's seat and away from him - Bryant fired three shots and killed her before she could escape.

Witnesses to the murder and abduction ran to hide in the trees that lined the back of the gas station. Inside, the clerk on duty at the station locked the front doors and told everyone inside to hide in the back of the store. Reaching under the counter, the clerk grabbed his own rifle and loaded the gun, but Bryant had already driven off in the BMW with Glenn Pears still locked in the trunk.

Within a few minutes, a police car pulled up in front of the gas station and the attendant told the officer about the gunman with long blond hair who took one man hostage and had killed the woman in the front seat of the car still parked in the entrance to the parking lot. The officer ran back to his squad car and began down the highway at full speed to try and catch up with the attacker.

Bryant was already well ahead of the police and was now parked in front of the tudor style Fox and Hounds resort hotel. Standing along the road, Bryant opened fire on several people standing outside the building as they ran for cover; having no idea what was going on or why a man was shooting at them. As a car approached from the other direction, Bryant turned and shot out the front windshield but failed to injure the occupants inside the vehicle.

A second vehicle driven by Michael Wanders was approaching the scene and slowed as they passed him thinking the man holding the rifle was hunting rabbits. The couple was shocked when the man pointed his rifle and began to shoot at them. As they tried to speed away to safety, a bullet cut through the throttle cable causing the car to lose power. Fortunately for the car's occupants, it was moving downhill and its forward momentum kept it rolling away as Bryant continued to fire at them - shattering the back windshield and hitting passenger Linda White in the arm.

As a third car approached oblivious as to what was happening, Bryant shattered the windshield of the car with his first shot, wounding Douglas Horner with broken glass. Instinctively, Horner stepped on the gas and tried to get away from the gunman. As they raced down the hill, they passed Michael Wanders and Linda White who were frantically waving at them in an effort to get them to stop. Their own car was stranded at the bottom of the hill barely out of the line of fire from where Bryant was standing. They sped past the couple before changing their mind at the last moment and quickly backed up, allowing the couple to get into the back seat before fleeing the bizarre situation to safety.

As traffic continued to drive past the gunman - most were completely unaware there was any danger until Bryant would shoot at them. Susan Williams was hit in the hand by a bullet as her husband Simon Williams drove past where the gunman was standing. The car behind them jammed on their brakes and immediately put the vehicle in reverse while Bryant fired at them but missed his target.

With no other targets in site, Bryant put his rifle on the seat beside him in the BMW and began driving towards Seascape and the house where he had killed his first two victims earlier in the day.

Chapter Seven:

# A Scene of Total Devastation

By the time Bryant reached Seascape it was just before 3 pm. Approximately 90 minutes had passed since he began his murderous rampage and police from Hobart had started to arrive at Port Arthur. The death count to this point was 34 people with another 23 suffering from serious injuries either caused by bullets or debris and shrapnel from the gun shots.

Bryant had arrived at the Seascape Inn and opened the trunk where Glen Pears was still being held. At gunpoint he directed the man into the building and handcuffed him to the staircase railing inside the hotel. He then calmly walked back out to the car and poured a jerry can of gas on it before lightning it on fire. Within seconds, the car was fully engulfed in flames. A few moments later, two patrolmen arrived on the scene after spotting the burning car.

Seeing the officers arrive, Bryant began to shoot at them from the front window of the B&B and in a matter of seconds, had both officers pinned down in a ditch unable to get to safer cover. Radioing in for help, they gave their location to the dispatch operator who immediately directed a large response team to the Inn; where it appeared the Port Arthur gunman was now holed up.

A half hour away In Port Arthur, tourists and staff remained cautiously hidden for fear that the gunman could still be outside and waited for the police to arrive from Hobart. As the sirens approached a sense of relief washed over the area; but there was still the apprehension of not knowing if the shooter was still in range. The entire country side was now on alert and awash in sirens and the sounds of helicopters arriving to the area. More than 200 police were dispatched to Port Arthur and ambulances began to pour into historical site.

To this point, police had very little information on who the gunman was – just that he had long blond hair and was in his mid to late twenties. The assault had happened so fast, that there were dozens of conflicting reports as to how tall the man was and what he looked like, as well as which direction he had headed. With Bryant now confirmed as the primary suspect in the shooting and now holed up in the Seascape house, police tactical response teams were able to focus on the specific area – although dozens of police remained in Port Arthur to ensure that there wasn't a second shooter or further threat to civilians.

As emergency responders arrived on scene of the museum bus parking lot and the Broad Arrow Café – little could have prepared them for what they would encounter. The scenic area had been turned into a war zone and there were more dead and wounded than was initially count reported. As police surrounded the area with guns drawn, first aid providers and paramedics raced to assess the dead from the living and to set up a make shift triage system to get the most severely wounded airlifted via helicopter back to the hospital in Hobart where they were preparing to receive for those that survived the attack.

Inside the café, dozens of people lay dead and blood covered the walls and floor. Bryant had been using metal jacket bullets that not only are capable of piercing through armored vehicles, but upon impact, the metal tipped head of the bullet explodes like a mushroom and does significant damage to whatever it hits. When struck by a bullet of this caliber and type, the result is mass tissue damage and fragmented bone which can splinter into deadly sharp shards. These bullets are unlike standard ammunition where loses velocity quickly when it strikes and the wound is often clean. Most that were shot by Bryant were either killed instantly or bled to death before rescuers could reach them.

At the Royal Hobart Hospital, Steve Wilkinson, head of special surgery was on shift and had received word that a major disaster had happened at Port Arthur and he was preparing for the wounded to start arriving momentarily. Information was scattered and there was no way to know how many injured people they would be dealing with. As the causalities started arriving, wounds ranged from shrapnel punctures to severely wounded individuals who had lost dangerous amounts of blood. Because of the massive amount of damaged or missing tissue – surgical teams worked frantically to save those that were already close to death.

Chapter Eight:

# The Cornered Madman

As police converged on Seascape and tightened their noose around Bryant inside the house, there was no way to know if the gunman had hostages inside the inn or if he was alone. As investigators had worked frantically to try and piece together information on the shooter's identity; was and word began to trickle in that the name of the shooter was likely a man named Martin Bryant. Bryant, was known to Tasmania police for his erratic behavior, including the incident where he was shooting his pellet gun at tourists near his farm in Copping.

By now the entire region was beginning to learn about the attack as word spread across Australia and the globe about the deadly shooting spree at one of the country's most famous historical sites – and the resulting standoff that was taking place between the shooter and Hobart police.

Lead negotiator Terry MacCarthy arrived at Seascape just before 3 pm to witness Bryant still shooting randomly at the officers who had begun to surround the property. However, they were careful to not expose themselves to the gun fire coming from inside the Inn.

To this point all MacCarthy knew was the likely name of the shooter and that conflicting reports had come in already from family members who suggested Bryant was suffering from schizophrenia. As the police set up a command post, MacCarthy dialed the phone number of the Inn several times in succession until the man inside picked up the phone.

"Hello" the voice on the other end of the phone answered with no sense of panic or fear. MacCarthy was taken back by the almost cheerful nature of the man's voice and disposition.

"Is this Martin?" MacCarthy asked.

"It's me Jamie" the man called himself as he responded with no hesitation. Jamie was a name Bryant had often referred to himself as.

"Jamie - How are things going in there"

"Oh couldn't be better – just like on a Hawaiian Holiday…" Bryant responded.

"A Hawaiian holiday?"

"Yes that's correct sir" Bryant's voice continued to be cheery and seemingly oblivious to the situation.

"I'm sorry I don't understand what you mean by that."

"I don't know myself... no?" Bryant sounded confused like he didn't understand his own words.

Although MacCarthy was the senior negotiator with decades of experience in dealing with hostile hostage situations, he was taken back by the whimsical disposition and words that were being said by Martin Bryant. It was clear they were not dealing with a typical hostage situation and that Bryant had no obvious or immediate demands - or even an apparent reason for what he had done.

With Bryant surrounded now at Seascape, the primary focus of the negotiations was to try and determine if there was any hostages inside the building. This would have a direct effect on how police tactical units handled the situation. If they could establish that no one else was inside the building, then they could focus on talking down the gunman without fear of him killing or hurting anyone else. If there were hostages, then an entirely different tactic would be required, including ensuring that nothing was done to aggravate the gunman any worse than he apparently already was.

No one had seen the Martins who owned and operated the Seascape Inn since early that morning, and there was an unconfirmed report of a man being taken hostage by Bryant in the trunk of the stolen BMW; which was still burning close by. Police had managed to check the vehicle and there was no sign of any one in the car. This meant that either Bryant had already dumped his hostage before arriving at the Inn – or the man was inside the building and being held captive. With the Martins and the kidnapped man unaccounted for, there were potentially three civilians inside that were trapped with their attacker - and this didn't take into account any potential guests or staff in the building that may be being held inside.

MacCarthy continued to talk with Bryant in an effort to gather information as well as the important task of keeping him distracted from shooting at the police outside. Careful attention was also being paid while talking with the gunman to any sounds of people in the background – of which there were none.

It was approaching seven o-clock and although Bryant had stopped shooting at police outside, he showed no apparent willingness to end the standoff. When negotiators quizzed him on how things were inside, he told police he was preparing dinner for his hostages; there was no way to be sure whether he was bluffing or telling the truth. As the conversation progressed, Bryant told MacCarthy he had been out surfing that afternoon and made no reference to the attack at Port Arthur.

As the sun gave way to night fall – Bryant became concerned by the police presence around the Inn and wanted to know why a police sniper had a rifle pointed at the house.

"What I've actually found out mannnn" he drawled out the word man "is that one of your boys is right outside – North East I'd say with an infrared scope – can you just ask him to move on?"

"We will do that" MacCarthy answered.

"He's gonna shoot your main man" Bryant answered with a hint of fear in his voice.

"Martin we have a real situation here – there was a terrible shooting at Port Arthur"

"Was anyone hurt?" Bryant quizzed.

"There were a number of people hurt"

"They weren't killed?" He asked – sounding almost disappointed that the negotiator said there were only injured people and no one dead.

"I don't know the full details."

As the verbal exchange continued, Bryant started to become more agitated and police suspected he had either run out of ammunition or was down to his last few rounds, especially since there hadn't been any shots fired in several hours.

"Martin, what do you say we end this and you put down your weapon and come outside" MacCarthy asked calmly.

"No I think I want a heli – you need to get me a heli here." Bryant demanded a helicopter be made available to him. "You can buy a heli." his voice was becoming more agitated. "I've got the money – don't you understand – I've got the money. I've got all the wealth I want"

"Alright"

"I want the heli now" he demanded.

It was then that negotiators ran into an unanticipated problem – the cordless phone they had been talking with Bryant on inside Seascape had lost its charge and the line went dead. There was no means now to continue to communicate with the agitated man and a decision needed to be made about what the next step was to be. A potential option was to storm the house and take Bryant by force, but they couldn't be sure that they could protect any hostages inside the building; despite their suspicions that there was no one else alive other than Bryant.

The other option was to simply wait him out until he came out on his own. There was no way of communicating with the police outside the Inn – but with no signs of anyone still alive in the building besides Bryant, police elected to wait until sunrise when they could better determine the next course of action.

As daylight broke on Monday, April 29th, Bryant had been in Seascape for 18 hours. The night had been quite and despite several attempts, no further communication took place with Bryant. Police had no idea as to what to expect next from a man who had become one of the most deadly killers in the world the previous day.

A tight perimeter had been established around the guest house and a constant watch ensured there was no chance or possibility he could escape.

Shortly before 8 am, smoke suddenly started to pour out of the main building. Authorities were shocked to realize that Bryant had apparently set the house on fire as flames began to become evident.

Within 10 minutes the house was becoming completely engulfed by fire. The front door burst open and Bryant - his clothes partially on fire - ran out and began to roll around on the front lawn of the Inn. Police immediately moved in and used a blanket to put the flames out on Bryant's body – and despite being badly burned, he was handcuffed and taken into custody.

Rescuers raced into the burning building, searching for any hostages that may be still alive. It was there they found the Martin's dead, as well as, the lone hostage Bryant had taken from the Mobil gas station, Glen Pierce – still handcuffed to the stair case railing of the house.

Martin Bryant's deadly rampage was finally at an end – and the gunman was now on his way to the same hospital where many of his victims were being treated. With severe burns to several parts of his body, the Burn Unit at the Royal Hobart Hospital now had to treat the injuries of the man who had killed 35 people less than 24 hours ago.

Chapter Nine:

# The Aftermath

Bryant had been seriously burned from the fire he had started at Seascape, but was now in stable condition and recovering in the hospital under tight security. Assigned to keep close watch on Martin Bryant was Officer Phil Pyke, who had first met the gunman several years earlier while assisting in the search for the missing Maurice Bryant.

Tensions ran high in the ward as several armed policeman stood guard outside the doors of the room the gunman was being held in. Bryant's long blond hair was a tangled melted mess and the smell of burnt skin hung heavily in the air. Hospital staff were told to use extreme caution when dealing with their now infamous patient who had already made several verbal threats towards nurses and had made shooting motions with his restrained hands as they walked by his bed.

The extent of the burns were severe enough to require netted bandages to try and keep the skin from falling off his body while it healed. Despite the injuries, he remained securely handcuffed at all times to the bed.

Bryant had been formally charged with the murders at Port Arthur and was in the official custody of the Australian Justice Department. Authorities had become concerned over the potential of vigilantes storming the hospital as several reports had come in to police headquarters of people flying in from around the country to even the score. Guards were told to remain vigilant for any individual that may try to attack the burn ward in an effort to get to Bryant. Officer Pyke had already decided in his own mind that if they were to try and attack the hospital – they could have Bryant and that his only job was to protect the nurses and doctors of the hospital.

No one was to have closer contact to the recovering gunman than Pyke. In his memoirs, he would later recall the way Bryant would flip from almost childlike behavior to that of an evil killer numerous times throughout the day. He would stare at the medical staff or guards with an lifeless, cold fixation and then just as quickly return to an almost helpless state of an injured 10 year old wanting to be comforted by the adults in the room.

As the investigation continued into the timeline and events of what had happened, word of the cold blooded execution of the young Mikac girls began to spread and Pyke stood over the bed of Bryant looking down on the man who had taken so many lives without a hint of remorse. Bryant opened his eyes and stared coldly up at him – Pyke tapped at his gun in his holster and said through gritted teeth "If you get out of those cuffs Martin – this is for you – as I can fight back unlike your other victims."

Throughout the week investigators continued to gather evidence as forensic teams examined the crime scenes in an attempt to determine what had happened. Bryant had fired more than 250 rounds of .308 steel tipped ammunition. Police recovered the AR 15 Assault Rifle in the back of his yellow Volvo and the FAL semi-automatic rifle in the burned out Seascape Inn. They also found a self-loading Korean made Daewoo combat shotgun with a large clear garbage bag full of hundreds of live shells.

Martin Bryant offered little assistance in understanding why he went on his rampage and denied that he remembered anything about what had taken place. This fit in with the suggestion from relatives that he was a suffering schizophrenic who had no recollection of what he had done.

By the time the investigation would be completed more than 1000 witnesses would have their statements taken as Crown Prosecutors prepared their case against Bryant. 35 people lay dead and 23 were injured in a case that shook the nation and shocked the world.

When Bryant was brought to trial, prosecutors laid out a detailed and shocking case that painstakingly examined how a lone gunman was able to murder so many people so quickly. It was no surprise when Bryant entered a plea of not guilty when the initial charges were read aloud. Day after day before the Australian Supreme Court, evidence was examined and were given that showed Bryant as a crazed killer with little remorse for his actions.

As the case wound down – Martin Bryant would once again shock the entire country when he changed his plea from not guilty to guilty which was accepted by the court.

There were few in Australia that didn't now wait for the sentence that would be handed down to what many saw as an unremorseful cold blooded killer – and the discussion over the death penalty being a fitting penalty gained traction. Australia did not have laws that supported capital punishment.

On the day of sentencing, Martin Bryant showed little emotion and there were those that questioned if he even understood what was happening. As he rose before the court the sentencing verdict was read out loud.

"Taking account of the medical evidence and of his lack of insight into the magnitude and effects of his conduct, apparent in all his appearances before this Court, I have no reason to hope and every reason to fear that he (the defendant) will remain indefinitely as disturbed and insensitive as he was when planning and executing the crimes of which he now stands convicted."

"Martin Bryant, on each of the 35 counts of murder in this indictment, you are sentenced to imprisonment for the term of your natural life. I order that you not be eligible for parole in respect of any such a sentence."

"On each of the remaining counts in the indictment, you are sentenced to imprisonment for 21 years, to be served concurrently with each other, and with the concurrent sentence of life imprisonment already imposed."

"In respect of each sentence of 21 years, I order that you likewise not be eligible for parole."

In total, Bryant was sentenced to 35 Life sentences for the people he killed - plus the penalties handed down for those he injured for a grand total of 1035 years.

He was remanded in Risdon Prison in Tasmania where he was to spend the rest of his life.

Chapter Ten:

# Understanding the Mind of a Killer

One of things so terrifying about rampage killers like Martin Bryant is the nature of their crime. Unlike a methodical serial killer who may kill dozens of people over an extended period – rampage killers attack without warning and within minutes can kill dozens of people, as in the case of Bryant or other shocking attacks, such as, the shootings at Columbine High School in Littleton, Colorado.

In a more recent attack, 12 people were killed and another 70 wounded when James Eagan Holmes opened fire in a crowded movie theater in Aurora, Colorado. By the time police could respond to the scene of the attack – the damage had already been done. For the families of those that were killed or those that were wounded in these types of attacks – there is no rhyme or reason – just a case of being in the right place at the wrong time.

In the case of Martin Bryant – there had been several tell-tale warning signs that he was a potentially violent offender, but in the 1990's, rampage killers were not as common as they are now and police were less likely to track or act on a potentially violent member of the community.

In the first 8 months of Bryant's confinement in the psychiatric ward of Risdon Penitentiary, doctors determined that there was little hope of ever rehabilitating the inmate. It was determined that he had the IQ of an 11 year old with very little interest, if any, in anyone but himself. Never the less, doctors and authorities wanted to learn more about what makes a killer like Martin Bryant tick.

Killers like Bryant are rarely safe from other inmates in a prison like Risdon and must be kept separated from those in general population. All of Australia – including some of the most violent imprisoned murderers in the entire country had heard of the execution of the two small children, and Bryant's likelihood of surviving more than a few days among other general population was very remote. To compound matters, Bryant was continually trying to commit suicide. A special cell was constructed from two previous cells to hold the inmate and protect him from both outside threats as well as himself.

Dr. Wilf Lopez was one of the doctors assigned to assess Bryant and knew within a few weeks of observing his behavior that there would be no expectation that Bryant was anything but a unremorseful, cold blooded killer who given the chance would kill again. The gunman showed no signs of regrets and would remind both medical staff and guards on a daily basis what he had done, wearing the title of the Nation's worst mass murdered as a badge of honor.

In one particularly alarming incident, Bryant asked a female nurse if she had children and then suggested it would be nice if she brought them by for a visit – followed by where he held his hand like a loaded gun and pointed at her making a "click click" noise as if to shoot them. In another incident, he offered a female guard his sperm so she could have his baby.

Such was the attitude in Australia that authorities had to take special precautions of ensure the safety of Bryant from guards, medical staff and support workers who were in contact with him in prison. There was a heightened fear that he would be poisoned by someone with access to his food and subsequently steps were taken to ensure that no one could attempt to kill him in this manner. The irony was lost on no one that special precautions needed to be considered to protect a man who had killed so many and now seemed to tremendously enjoy his own notoriety.

Ever since the sentence was handed down, there had been pressure from the public as well as government officials that Bryant should receive no special protection while in prison – or as much protection as his victims did when he attacked them.

Then serving Attorney General Ray Groom promised the public that Bryant would not be protected from other inmates his whole life in prison and one day "would pay the price of what he had done and that is what will occur".

In studying and observing Bryant there is little evidence to suggest he has any remorse or empathy for those he hurt or what he had done. The court had already ruled that he was not insane, although his behavior often indicated elsewise. In a country with no death penalty, the ruling of the Supreme Court had the final say and prison authorities were now charged with managing the imprisonment of the killer.

There have been many who have attempted to understand why Martin Bryant became a brutal, cold blooded rampage killer. Psychologists have spent nearly two decades studying him with the hope of determining a pattern and warning signs to identify future potential killers.

Even as a young child Bryant showed signs of being a violent individual with a fascination of death and harming others. Ever since he was in his earliest years of development he had little ability to fit in with others and his erratic and odd behavior made it difficult for others to relate to him. Through his childhood years he was prone to playing odd pranks on others, but as he grew older, the pranks became darker and more disconcerting to those around him, including local authorities.

As an adult, Bryant's behavior reached new levels of oddity. His father was forced to take on the role of full time restrainer in order to protect Bryant from harming himself or others. It was clear that his son's behavior was becoming worse and his social skills were diminishing. When Maurice Bryant died, there was no one left to keep him from sinking deeper into depravity.

In retrospect is seemed obvious that the adult Bryant was always a threat to the public. In the years leading up to the attack on Port Arthur, he was rarely seen not carrying his air rifle and there were repeated complaints about him shooting at people, animals and cars.

The loss of his best friend Helen Harvey was a severe blow to the already mental wellbeing of Bryant. After the car accident that had killed the woman, his own recovery was slow and painful from the injuries he sustained, including two shattered vertebras in his neck. His behavior began to become more abusive and he started to become a problem to the local neighborhood children whom he would pester and bully during their playtime.

By his own admission Martin Bryant sought help for his increasingly deep sense of despair following the death of Helen Harvey. He complained of a growing sense of anxiety and constant sadness. He was prescribed a tricyclic antidepressant.

When Bryant's father was found dead, despite the concerns of those around him that he may have played a role in his death, police found enough evidence to indicate that Maurice Bryant did take his own life. Martin Bryant's bizarre and jovial behavior at the farm where the body of his father was found was attributed to his inability to understand consequences and was a poignant example of his limited comprehension of even the most basic social behaviors.

Outside of proving the basic necessities of life – there is no policy on what comforts and privileges must be provided to a prisoner like Bryant, and thus, his existence is sparse. He is allowed a radio that is out of his reach in his cell, but is allowed no access to the outside world or news media and in particular any knowledge of how the country has reacted to his crimes.

As the years have passed since Martin Bryant was imprisoned, there has been little change in his daily routine. He exercises twice a day with a program he created for himself which resembles a form of dancing and jumping jacks. He occasionally builds puzzles but is allowed no access to anything he could use to harm himself or others. In the nearly two decades behind bars, he has attempted to commit suicide 6 times and is now watched by three cameras 24 hours a day. His suicide attempts include once trying to hang himself with his bed sheet on the end of his bed, as well as, trying to swallow a tube of toothpaste that then became lodged in his throat.

Because of his limited intelligence and mental state, there is very little in the line of traditional activities that can be offered to him as an inmate. There is no education he can participate in that is at his diminished level of learning ability, and there is no usual function he can provide in a work related environment.

An entire generation of medical staff and prison employees has come and gone since Martin Bryant was locked up. Today, there are few in the prison that remember when he first arrived. He now keeps his head shaved and refuses to receive any visitors including his mother who has campaigned for years that the government should look into the conspiracy theories that her son was not the killer that day in Port Arthur.

Bryant still has little to discuss with anyone, other than wanting to talk about his murderous rampage and how famous of a man he had become. Over the years he has had more privileges added to his schedule, including limited access to social situations with other inmates, such as playing table tennis. He is allowed to exercise and go outside in a caged area of the court yard but is still protected from the general population.

Martin John Bryant is eligible for release in the year 3032.

# Epilogue

Following that fatal warm April day in 1996 when Martin John Bryant left so many people dead in such a short time, the Australian government was quick to move on what it saw as a situation that made it far too easy for a man like Martin Bryant to purchase powerful weapons capable of causing such damage to innocent people. Here was a man with the IQ and mentality of a child able to purchase, at will, military issue weapons capable of inflicting incredible pain and carnage. There was no checks and balances or a system to prevent a man like Bryant from stocking up on large quantities of ammunition.

In what would become a text book model solution to the issue of assault rifles being held by the general public, the Australian authorities created a program called the National Fire Arms Agreement; where a ban was placed on all automation and semi-automatic weapons despite the protests of the gun lobby movement who accused authorities of using the Port Arthur tragedy to legislate gun control laws in order to evoke martial law across the nation.

To encourage gun owners to turn in their banned weapons, it was decided that the government would buy back these weapons, leading to more than 750,000 guns were turned in.

It wasn't long after the guilty plea by Bryant that rumors began to circulate that a conspiracy had taken place in order to bring in the new, stricter gun laws. Conspiracy theories abounded that there was more than one gunman and that Bryant was just a patsy; who was an agent of the government or the fall guy for the Prime Minister's desire to outlaw assault rifles.

Those that survived the massacre tell a much more pointed story. Survivor Peter Croswell scoffs at those that suggest Bryant didn't kill the 20 people in the Broad Arrow Café and those that suggest he was innocent are wrong - stating that he saw with his own eyes Bryant shoot the patrons in the café.

Security manager Ian Kingston has stronger words for those that suggest Bryant was innocent or not the shooter.

"I don't know where all this crap came from that was put out – it's all a lot of bull shit" He says with total conviction. "I was there in the middle of it and I know exactly what happened. I don't know where these stories originate you know – but it's a load of rubbish"

There are those that point to the accuracy of which the shooter was able to hit his targets and the questions as to whether a man of Bryant's mental capacity could have achieved the same results – Bryant had carried a rifle in his hands since he was 14 years old and had shot at targets his whole life with various weapons. Outside of a real guns recoil – the nature of aiming any weapon remains the same and he was a proficient marksman.

There is little doubt or evidence to suggest that he was anything but the lone killer at Port Arthur and Seascape, despite the numerous blogs and articles suggesting that a mass conspiracy took place on behalf of the Australian Government, the court system, law enforcement officials and the more than 1000 statements taken by eye witnesses including those that clearly identified him as the lone shooter. It seems rather improbable that so many people would willingly go along with such a conspiracy – all content to serve the will of authorities and their pursuit of new gun control laws rather than find and prosecute the true killer(s) at Port Arthur.

Conspiracy theories aside, with what is now known about Martin Bryant and his troubled childhood, as well as, his inability to cope in society as an adult, the complex question of his ability to understand his crimes and his subsequent punishment come into question. At the time of his trial, there was immense political pressure to refuse the notion that he was not fit to stand trial on the grounds of insanity. The entire nation demanded that Bryant pay for his crimes and with emotions so high, there would have been absolute outrage if he had been found not guilty of the murders he committed. What is clear however, is that although he was an adult – his mentality was that of a child in grade 5, he suffered from severe bouts of anger, an inability to deal with his actions – or to understand the consequences of them.

It is part of the lack of ability to understand the consequences of his actions that has made Bryant impossible to rehabilitate. Those that have observed him have noted that his only recollection of the events at Port Arthur are those that he has either been told about or read about. Subsequently, he has assumed, and relished in the role of being the crazed gunman and the notoriety he gained from it – despite not being able to recall doing it.

This brings into question the logic of treating Bryant as an individual capable of grasping what he has done and the punishment that he has been sentenced to. Without doubt he is an unremorseful, dangerous killer as he proved at Port Arthur and that he remains a threat to those around him to this day. The man in prison has assumed the role of a mass murderer and gunman, and that is part of what makes him so dangerous; besides the evidence, that he at any moment is capable of horrible atrocities against his fellow man – despite his inability to understand his actions.

***

The Broad Arrow Café was demolished and a memorial garden was created on the site as a means to remember those that lost their lives on the 28th of April, 1996.

Martin John Bryant remains in solitary confinement in Tasmania's maximum security Brisbane Penitentiary.

# More books by Jack Rosewood

In an area of Houston known as the Heights, boys had been going missing for years, but it was the peace-and-love 1970s, so police just called them runaways, even if they'd left with little more than a swimsuit and some change.

When the truth was uncovered, and police – and the rest of Houston – realized the boys had become victims of notorious American serial killer Dean Corll, Houston recoiled in horrified shock. Residents realized that they had not only become the site of the most grisly mass murder in Texas history, but the worst mass murder in all of U.S. history.

The word serial killer had not yet been coined, and as body after decomposing body was uncovered from the dirt floor of the boat shed where Corll and his two young accomplishes had buried most of the victims, there were hardly words for what this sadistic lust killer had done. The depraved evil that Corll and his accomplices – two teen boys themselves who were promised money but eventually developed a thrill for the kill - was revealed as one of the cohorts, Wayne Henley, calmly, affably, told the stories of how after Corll sexually assaulting them and tortured them in unimaginable fashion, they would kill them and take the boys' bodies away to bury them beneath the dirt.

This serial killer's biography will haunt you, especially as you learn more about the sadistic torture methods lust killer Corll used on his young victims, all lured to his various apartments by people they believed were their friends.

While Corll is dead, killed by Henley during the lust killer's last night of depravity, the case remains entwined in Houston history, and unforgettable for the families of those who lived it.

When Chris Bryson was discovered nude and severely beaten stumbling down Charlotte Street in Kansas City in 1988, Police had no idea they were about to discover the den of one of the most sadistic American serial killers in recent history. This is the true historical story of Robert Berdella, nicknamed by the media the Kansas City Butcher, who from between 1984 and 1988 brutally raped, tortured and ultimately dismembered 6 young male prostitutes in his unassuming home on a quiet street in Kansas City.

Based on the actual 720 page detailed confession provided by Berdella to investigators, it represents one of the most gruesome true crime stories of all time and is unique in the fact that it details each grizzly murder as told by the killer himself. From how he captured each man, to the terrifying methods he used in his torture chamber, to ultimately how he disposed of their corpses - rarely has there ever been a case where a convicted serial killer confessed to police in his own words his crimes in such disturbing detail.

Horrific, shocking and rarely equaled in the realms of sadistic torture – Berdella was a sexually driven lust killer and one of the most sadistic sex criminals ever captured. Not for the faint of heart, this is the tale of Robert "Bob" Berdella, the worst serial killer in Kansas City History and for those that are fans of historical serial killers, is a true must read.

Richmond, Virginia: On the morning of October 19, 1979, parolee James Briley stood before a judge and vowed to quit the criminal life. That same day, James met with brothers Linwood, Anthony, and 16-year-old neighbor Duncan Meekins. What they planned—and carried out—would make them American serial-killer legends, and reveal to police investigators a 7-month rampage of rape, robbery, and murder exceeding in brutality already documented cases of psychopaths, sociopaths, and sex criminals.

As reported in this book, the Briley gang were responsible for the killing of 11 people (among these, a 5-year-old boy and his pregnant mother), but possibly as many as 20. Unlike most criminals, however, the Briley gang's break-ins and robberies were purely incidental—mere excuses for rape and vicious thrill-kills. When authorities (aided by plea-bargaining Duncan Meekins) discovered the whole truth, even their tough skins crawled. Nothing in Virginian history approached the depravities, many of which were committed within miles of the Briley home, where single father James Sr. padlocked himself into his bedroom every night.

But this true crime story did not end with the arrests and murder convictions of the Briley gang. Linwood, younger brother James, and 6 other Mecklenburg death-row inmates, hatched an incredible plan of trickery and manipulation—and escaped from the "state-of-the-art" facility on May 31, 1984. The biggest death-row break-out in American history.

# A Note From The Author

Hello, this is Jack Rosewood. Thank you for reading Martin Bryant: The Port Arthur Massacre. I hope you enjoyed the read of this chilling story. If you did, I'd appreciate if you would take a few moments to post a review on Amazon.

Thanks again for reading this book, make sure to follow me on Facebook at Jack Rosewood Author.

Best Regards

Jack Rosewood

Printed in Poland
by Amazon Fulfillment
Poland Sp. z o.o., Wrocław